ASHDOWN FOREST

AN ILLUSTRATED GUIDE
BY PHILIP J. GLYN AND
HEW D. V. PRENDERGAST

ESSEDON PRESS

One of the Forest's 'clear running brooks', just north east of the Ashdown Forest Centre.

Two series of iron milestones, showing the distance from London, cross the Forest: on the A22 and the B2026. This milestone, near the Roman Road car park (473293), was erected in 1767 by the Westerham and Edenbridge Trust which managed the road.

Introduction

After crossing Ashdown Forest in 1822, William Cobbett famously described it in his agricultural treatise *Rural Rides* as 'a heath, with here and there a few birch scrubs upon it, verily the most villainously ugly spot I ever saw in England'. A more sympathetic view was expressed by Mr A.E. Knox in 1849. 'Nothing can exceed the picturesque beauty of certain portions of this district' he wrote in *Ornithological Rambles in Sussex*: 'eminences clothed with heather and gorse, and crowned with Scotch fir and holly, enclose valleys intersected by clear running brooks, whose course, here rapid and noisy, rushes over rocks and ridges of sandstone'. A century and a half later the 'picturesque beauty' is still there, just 70 kilometres from central London, in a rare open space that has also become a refuge for specialised and increasingly threatened wildlife.

Shaped originally by climate and geology, the landscape of the Forest has been modified by millennia of human activity. There have been hunting and grazing, the felling of timber and the production of iron. Britons, Romans and Saxons all left their mark. Then came the Normans. The Forest of today retains much of the identity they gave it, due largely to the determination of its Commoners to defend their rights to its resources.

Today, however, there are new pressures. A million and more visitors every year bring cars, dogs, litter, fire and trampling feet to the Forest; Bracken and birches invade its heathland; and new road schemes are seldom far away.

This guide is an introduction to the Forest's rich past and present and to what is worth seeing and conserving. We define the Forest as all that land within its original boundary; about half of it, however, has been in private hands since 1693 and has little or no public access. We strongly recommend buying the local Ordnance Survey (O.S.) Pathfinder maps (1247, 1248, and 1269) and visiting the Ashdown Forest Centre east of Wych Cross (grid reference TQ 432324).

The influence of geology

The existence of the Forest owes much to events that began about 130 million years ago, in the Lower Cretaceous period. According to one recent theory, the area was covered at the time by rivers crossing a vast flood plain. The deposits they laid down are known collectively as the Hastings Beds. The lower 200 metres of this formation are the Ashdown Beds which consist mainly of fine sands, silts, siltstones and sandstones. They are covered by up to 70 metres of Wadhurst Clay. Among its grey shales are thin layers of limestone and sandstone, along with the ironstone which provided much of the iron ore for the Wealden iron industry. Fossils are common, notably of the dinosaur *Iguanadon* (first discovered near Cuckfield) and the horsetail *Equisetites lyelli* (named after one of geology's greatest nineteenth-century figures, Sir Charles Lyell).

These deposits were then buried and compacted by later ones, including some 300 metres of the marine-derived Chalk that now forms the North and South Downs. About 65 million years ago the whole of the Weald was forced up into a dome 1000 metres high. This has subsequently eroded away to reveal the Ashdown Beds and Wadhurst Clay that underlie and give rise to the soils of the Forest floor today.

The soils in turn interact with vegetation and man's management of it. Well-drained brown earths, rich in humus, support deciduous woodland. Poor, grey, acidic soils (podzols) have developed under the Forest heathlands. Because of an impermeable layer of iron oxides, at some depth in the ground, they can easily become waterlogged.

Geological cross section of Ashdown Forest and the North and South Downs; all land below the dotted lines has been eroded away. The highest point of Ashdown Forest today is by Greenwood Gate Clump (474311), 223m above sea level.

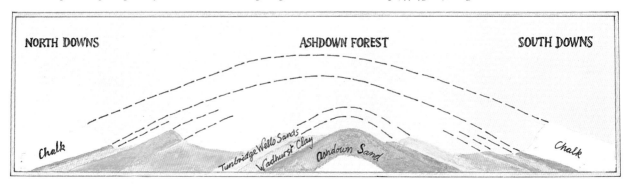

Archaeology

Only a trained or lucky eye finds signs of man's earliest occupations of Ashdown Forest: flint flakes of the Mesolithic and succeeding Neolithic and Bronze Age Periods (from about 8000 to 550BC). In the Forest Centre, however, there is an axe from the Palaeolithic Period perhaps 40–50,000 years old, long before the last ice sheets retreated from Britain.

More evident later remains are marked on the local Pathfinder maps. Although the TUMULUS south of Gills Lap (468312) may be Bronze Age, the FORT east of Ashdown Park (445319) is certainly Iron Age and dates from about 50BC. There was a later Roman Villa at the same site but the clearest imprint on the Forest of the time is the ROMAN ROAD that is seen best by the car park of that name (473294). The EARTHWORK (413309) north of Chelwood Gate is also late Iron Age and is some kind of enclosure; so too is the ENCLOSURE (that has not yet been excavated; 474313) south east of Gills Lap.

By far the most extensive and historically significant construction on the Forest was the 55 kilometre long pale that was built to surround it, and to contain its deer, in the thirteenth or fourteenth century. Its remnants are not shown on the O.S. maps but they are readily visible, especially near Legsheath Farm (402336). Here the ancient pale and the present Forest boundary are almost exactly coincident. Access to the Forest was by more than 40 gates or hatches; the names of some of them, such as Chelwood Gate and Coleman's Hatch, are still in use.

The archaeological remains most frequently indicated on the maps are PILLOW MOUNDS. Most of the seven sites lie in the northern half of the Forest from Hindleap in the west (405322) to Church Hill in the east (493324) and date from the late seventeenth century. These mounds, made of turf and up to 200 metres long and seven metres wide, were for the rearing of rabbits whose fur and meat were valuable commodities. Just how valuable is shown by the extensive areas still known as warrens (Broadstone, Crowborough, Wych, Wren's and Hindleap itself) and by court appearances such as that of William Rogers at Duddleswell in 1651 'for killing and destroying many coneys in the forest'. (The word 'coney' has long since been replaced by 'rabbit' in British English but usage continues in North America.)

Other names bear witness to further important activities on the Forest. Kings Standing (475304) is believed to be the site of a stand or hide past which deer were driven and then ambushed during hunts in Tudor times. Camp Hill (469289) was the site of a military camp in 1793 although the name itself goes back to at least 1564. During both World Wars the openness of the Forest proved an ideal place for exercise and manoeuvres, a military practice that continues today in the Ministry of Defence (M.o.D.) training area adjacent to Pippingford Park. The Second World War saw also the construction of aerials above Duddleswell to broadcast BBC services to Europe and propaganda to the enemy. The nuclear age has left its imprint with an underground bunker on the same site.

A pillow mound on M.o.D. heathland. This is one of the Forest's Scheduled Ancient Monuments.

Ashdown Forest, from a 1610 map of Sussex, with its boundary, the pale, clearly marked as a fence. Whiteden and Cornbed were both hunting lodges. The Parliament Commissioners report on the Forest in 1650 said that 'All that . . . impald ground commonly called ye great Pike of Lancaster or the fforest of Ashdowne . . . doth contain by admeasurement 13391 acres and 27 perches' – about 5420 hectares.

Documented history

By far the greatest length of the Forest's history is recorded on and in the ground alone. With the arrival of the Normans, however, not only did this change, with the writing of documents, but for the first time events can be related to individuals rather than merely peoples.

To the Saxon predecessors of the Normans, Ashdown was apparently an unnamed part of a far greater forest called Andredswald that stretched 200 kilometres from west to east and 50 kilometres from north to south. Ashdown is not mentioned in the Domesday Book of 1086 (unlike other forests such as the New Forest and the Forest of Dean) but, lying as it did within the Rape of Pevensey, it had already been granted by William the Conqueror to his half brother Robert. There were, however, two crucial conditions concerning rights: that the King could keep (and hunt) deer on the Forest and that the Commoners could continue to use it in their customary way.

Ashdown's subsequent history is punctuated by some key events involving crown, nobility and Commoners. Despite being the least powerful group, the Commoners always had a strong voice and their identities, activities and grievances are recorded in detail in the Forest archives. Attention to this detail played a great part in the court cases of the late nineteenth century whose legacy is the Forest of today.

1229   Michelham Priory near Hailsham was founded by Gilbert de Aquila and endowed with grazing rights at Chelwood Vachery (432301; 'vaccary' is supposed to derive from the French for 'cow-house' or 'byre').

1372   Edward III granted the Forest of Ashdon (as it was spelled) to his third son John of Gaunt, the Duke of Lancaster. The Duke visited the Forest just once, in the autumn of 1381 soon after the quelling of the Peasants' Revolt. After his death in 1399, the Forest reverted to the Crown until the Restoration of 1660 when Charles II ascended the throne. During these three centuries the Forest was known as Lancaster Great Park.

1561   Sir Richard Sackville was granted the 'mastership of the Forest and keepership of the wild beasts therein'. Later, Sackvilles became Earls and Dukes of Dorset (hence the DORSET ARMS pubs in East Grinstead and Withyham) and they retained the Lordship of the Manor of Duddleswell (which included the Forest) until the extinction of the male line in 1815. They were followed by the related de la Warr family in whose hands the Forest stayed until 1988.

1650 After the turbulent and lawless years of the Civil War, the Commonwealth Parliament appointed Commissioners to produce a detailed report on the Forest. Its timber, for example, was valued at £620 and its deer at £120.

1689 Tension arising out of plans to enclose the Forest led to a lawsuit by the Earl of Dorset and his lessees against John Newnham and other Commoners. Four years later, a specially appointed commission arbitrated that 6400 acres should be left for the use of the Commoners whilst the remainder of the 13991 acres could be enclosed and improved. The Commoners were stripped of all their customary rights on the enclosures.

1876 John Miles, tenant of Posingford Farm at Chuck Hatch, was seen cutting litter on the Forest by William Pilbeam, a keeper working for Lord de la Warr. Miles's challenge to the Earl's instructions earlier that year that Commoners should cease such an activity led to a lengthy trial in the High Court of Justice. The Commoners lost, despite a well-laid defence and detailed historical research by a solicitor from Battle, William Raper. An appeal in 1881, however, found in their favour and in 1885 a Board of Conservators was established by Act of Parliament to oversee the Forest bye-laws, including the protection of Commoners' rights. This act also recognised the establishment of numerous small, hitherto illegal, enclosures on the Forest.

1988 With contributions from a number of sources, including a public appeal, East Sussex County Council bought the freehold of Ashdown Forest (Lordship of the Manor) from the Executors of the 10th Earl de la Warr and established the Ashdown Forest Trust as the Forest's owner. Management is supervised by the Board of Conservators which has sixteen members: eight are appointed by East Sussex County Council and two by Wealden District Council, five are elected by the Commoners and one represents the Lord of the Manor (i.e. the Ashdown Forest Trust). Day to day running of the Forest is carried out by the Forest Superintendent and a team of Rangers.

Newbridge Mill, looking up towards Gills Lap in about 1900. This part of the Forest, like many others, was much more open then than it is today.

1289 '*2000 lathes of timber in hand in the Forest of Essedon* — *2/-*
150 props made in the same forest — *8d*
for carriage of the same to the Castle with one cart — *8d*
400 boards of beech for panelling the Chapel made from
timber in hand in Assedon — *16d.*'

This was part of a bill for repairs to the Chapel of Pevensey Castle. The Castle guarded the coast of the Rape of Pevensey, one of six rapes into which Sussex was divided administratively by the Normans.

1297-1298. 'Account of Ralph de Saurel Keeper of the Honor of Aquila in the County of Sussex . . . in the 25th year of the reign of King Edward . . . Forest of Esshedon. The same renders account of £17. os. 11d. of the pannage of 1892 hogs and 355 pigs of strangers agisted in the Forest.' In Ashdown, pannage (the food of pigs in woods) was mainly Beech mast and, less importantly, acorns. 'Agisted' refers to the hiring of rights for grazing pigs to those who were not Commoners.

1350, 20 October. 'Know ye that whereas Phillippa Queen of England . . . lately granted to our beloved Thomas . . . de Berkhame and to William Fishide ten loads of a suitable brushwood to wit of beeches, oaks and birches . . . to be taken and carried by view and livery of the keeper of our same consort of that Forest . . . '

1520, 10 October. 'This is the cleyme of us the Kingsese Costomarye Tenantes by the othe that we made unto the Kynge . . . at the coorte holden at Notleye of all the clayme that we doe clayme of the Kyngese Grownde within the Forest of Ashdowne . . . none of the Foresters neyther any other ofycer oughte not to medle nor dryve any manere of Cattell of the Costomarye tenants within the Kyngese foreste . . . for it is our comone apendante and hathe been tyme out of minde . . . ' The Commoners ('Costomarye Tenantes') fight back.

1651, 25 November. At the Woodmote Court, Duddleswell. 'We present . . . Joseph Ebbes for enclosing upon the Fforest ground; . . .

Minutes of the first meeting of the Conservators and BELOW: *an extract from a later meeting, reporting transgressions of Forest byelaws.*

John Brook for cutting and carrieing away of the fforest one load of bushes he having no custome; . . . the Lord of the Manor of Duddleswell for maintaining a pound in the Forest and also for not maintaining the outer boundaries of the said forest . . .' The Woodmote Court was a legal system inherited from the Saxons for dealing with transgressions of Forest law and with admission of cattle and pigs onto the Forest.

1679, 11 April. 'Proposals made by the King's Grantees concerning the inclosing of Ashdown Forest to such as claim common of pasture there. The King was Lord and owner both of the soils and woods within the said Park or Forest and therefore might by law depasture feed or stock the same with deer coneys and any other sort of cattle whatsoever . . . The King did usually keep and depasture on the same about 3 or 4,000 head of Deer Red and Fallow and 3,000 head of cattle were usually taken in every year and maintained there as agistment in the King's right besides a great number of coneys in each of the 6 walkes.' Such a large number of deer seems unlikely. Was it a deliberate exaggeration?

1807, 20 April. 'Ashdown Forest. This is to give notice that no person is permitted to cut or carry off any litter from the said Forest or to cut or carry off any Turf or peat therefrom except such turf or peat as the parish officers . . . are desirous of cutting for the use of the poor of such parishes . . . on paying sixpence per load for turf and six pence per thousand for peat to William Garret of Withyham Bailiff to His Grace the Duke of Dorset Lord of the Manor of Duddleswell.'

1874, 21 August.

'To W.A. Raper Esq.

My dear Sir, Ashdown Forest. I saw Lord de la Warr about a month since on other subjects and took the opportunity of bringing before him your proposal for an Association to protect the Commoners rights on Ashdown Forest. Lord de la Warr sees no objection to your proposal and you may consider that the Association has his moral support but . . . you will not of course expect him to contribute to the expenses.

Yours truly for Partner and Self,
E.A. Nicholson.'

Iron working: the great Forest industry

It is hard to imagine this late sixteenth century view of the Weald penned by William Cambden: 'Full of iron mines it is in sundry places, where for the making and fining whereof there bee furnaces on every side, and a huge deale of wood is yearely spent, to which purpose divers brookes in many places are brought to runne in one chanell, and sundry medowes turned into pooles and waters, that they might bee of power sufficient to drive hammer milles, which beating upon the iron, resound all over the places adjoyning.'

The well-preserved stretch of Roman Road on the Forest (473293). It was built in about AD 100 to connect the iron-producing area of the Weald with London and was surfaced with cinder waste.

A small iron-stained stream near the Forest Centre.

Iron ore had been extracted from the Weald since pre-Roman times and processed in bloomeries. Inside a small furnace, fuelled usually by charcoal and fanned by some sort of bellows, a lump of impure but malleable iron was obtained; the molten waste material – slag – emerged from the base. In 1496 at Newbridge (marked by POND BAY; 454325), Britain's very first blast furnace was built. This process was a great technological advance on the bloomery, its main product being molten metal that could be poured straight into a mould or cast. Production was far greater and less laborious but it did require the harnessing of considerable water power to drive either the furnace bellows or the hammer of the adjoining forge, or both. The valleys of the Forest, together with its locally high rainfall, were especially suitable for the damming of streams to provide water power.

Because of conflict, particularly that of England with Spain, the Wealden iron industry reached its peak during Cambden's time. It had already established its reputation with the casting of the first iron cannon in England in 1543 (at Buxted, just south east of the Forest). For a further two centuries it enjoyed an almost complete national monopoly in cannon manufacture (the name of Boringwheel Mill Farm (457265) near Nutley derives from the process of boring a cannon's barrel). There have even been mischievous claims that both opposing fleets were armed with Wealden products when the Armada sailed up the Channel! In the eighteenth century Britain's iron industry moved to the Midlands where coke, rather than charcoal, was a far cheaper fuel. The last Wealden furnace closed in 1824. Apart from cannon, the best-known products of the furnaces are fire-backs and the iron gravestones in local churchyards (for example, at St Margaret's in West Hoathly).

At Newbridge all that remain are the hammerpond banks and a reminder in the name of the nearby Furnace Farm. There is also little left at the sites of other of the Forest's blast furnaces at Pippingford (IRONWORKS; 450316. The nearby IRONWORKS (446313) refers to a Roman bloomery.) and near Friar's Gate (POND BAY; 496322), though here the dam wall is an impressive 150 metres long. Elsewhere on the Forest glassy slag and cinder can still be found on the ground or in the bed of some streams while many of the streams themselves (and, by definition at least, those springs marked on the maps as CHALYBEATE; e.g. at 403329) continue to be stained by iron compounds.

Commoners with ancient rights

Although Ashdown Forest is owned by East Sussex County Council, it is also a registered area of common land over which 730 Commoners can exercise certain rights – rights which over the centuries have been threatened, disputed and defended. Rights are attached to land near the Forest, rather than to people or houses, and give an insight into the lives of local people in the past. Entitlements to current Commoners' rights were all registered under the Commons Registration Act of 1965. Land which was not re-registered then has lost commonable entitlement forever.

Brakes and litter: the right to cut bracken, heather and litter for the principal purpose of bedding down animals in winter. 'Brake' is a shortening of Bracken and 'litter' refers to other plants such as heathers, grass and rushes. These were important and jealously guarded resources.

Estovers: (derived from an Old French word for 'to be necessary') the right to cut Birch, Alder and Willow for use on the ancestral hearth.

Pasture and herbage: grazing rights whose extent is governed by the size of the commonable holding. Holdings of less than two acres can graze one sheep only but larger ones can graze 10 sheep per acre (to a maximum of 150) and two cattle per acre (to a maximum of 30). Holdings of greater than 50 acres can also graze a mill, or working, horse.

Voting for Conservators: Commoners can vote for Conservators and stand to become one themselves.

Bracken – once so useful, now widely regarded as a pest.

How the Rights of Common are exercised is subject to local bye-laws and under the control of the Conservators. Estovers, for example, may be cut only in designated areas, often where tree clearance is needed anyway. Each Commoner is entitled annually to two cords of wood (a cord being a stack of wood measuring 8ft x 4ft x 4ft). Due to changes in the economy and to the dangers posed by traffic to livestock, grazing rights on the open, unenclosed Forest have not been exercised since the removal of sheep in 1985. Far from losing interest in grazing issues, however, the Commoners continue to debate and influence the introduction of fenced enclosures for livestock.

A Commoner on horseback rounding up sheep in 1981.

The Forest heathlands and their plants

Its openness and beauty, as well as some of Britain's rarest wildlife, give heathland a high and affectionate profile for many people. Ashdown Forest has some 770 hectares of it, two to five per cent of all that is left in Britain, and one of the largest expanses in south east England. A further 600 hectares are covered by Bracken and grassland.

Heathland is characterised by the overwhelming abundance of plants in the heather family, especially Ling but also Bell Heather and Cross-leaved Heath. It occurs on poor, largely sandy soils and has been created

Sawwort on the mown verges of the Stonehill Road near Nutley Windmill.

Flowering Dwarf Gorse and heathers.

by centuries of grazing, woodland clearance and other forms of management by man. The heathland flora amongst the heathers, though not rich in numbers of plants, is highly characteristic. Among the commoner species are Tormentil, Heath Milkwort and Heath Bedstraw while the dominant grass is Purple Moor-grass. Other than the heathers themselves, the main shrubs are two species of gorses. Common Gorse can grow into impenetrable thickets to the almost complete exclusion of everything else and flowers from the depths of winter to early summer. Dwarf Gorse, much smaller and with paler green branches and leaves, flowers from mid-summer into autumn. Together the two species lend a botanical accuracy to the popular expression 'kissing is out of favour when gorse is out of bloom'! The heathlands are at their best in August: the heathers themselves are in full bloom and the air is heavy with their scent and humming with bees.

For many heathland specialities the Forest is their Sussex stronghold. Among the first to bloom, in May, is Petty Whin, a small, spiny shrub with yellow pea-flowers. At the same time the Creeping Willow (rarely taller than a metre) is producing an abundance of its seed-bearing fluff. The Heath Spotted Orchid is out in June. As summer progresses botanical interest shifts to the damper parts of the heaths and to bogs and seepage lines - such as those just east of the Isle of Thorns at Chelwood Gate. In July these areas are often best located by the brilliant yellow displays of Bog Asphodel or by the sedges, Common Cottongrass (Bog Cotton) and

Creeping Willow near Millbrook.

Petty Whin near Millbrook.

Marsh Gentian near Millbrook.

Oblong-leaved Sundew near the Ashdown Forest Centre.

White-beaked Sedge. They may also contain two species of 'carnivorous' plants, the Common Sundew and the rarer Oblong-leaved Sundew. The Royal Fern grows at the Isle of Thorns.

The bogs are also rich in non-flowering plants such as many species of *Sphagnum* mosses and a diverse assortment of other mosses and liverworts. One remarkable occurrence, in two different stream sites, is that of *Nardia compressa*, a liverwort typical of the wetter uplands of western and northern Britain that has survived in the relatively damp climate of the Weald. Marsh Clubmoss is restricted now to just one site on the Forest.

Ashdown Forest's most famous plant is the Marsh Gentian. As long ago as 1890, a Sussex correspondent pleaded in a journal oddly named *Hardwicke's Science-Gossip*: 'It is to be hoped that all local naturalists will do their best to prevent this rare and beautiful plant from becoming extinct.' If it was scarce then, it is even scarcer now. It disappeared from West Sussex in the 1950s but on the Forest it is still quite abundant in about a dozen colonies. It has, furthermore, a long flowering season from July to well into October and its bright blue trumpet flowers are easy enough to find though they require sunny conditions to open fully.

Some plants are known to have disappeared from the Forest. For example W.H. Coleman, in his *Flora of East Grinstead* written in 1836, gave the last known occurrence of Juniper – even then it was 'very scarce'. The Bog Orchid has not been seen since 1952 and the Hairy Greenweed (a nationally rare species) not since 1979. It is precisely to prevent the disappearance of other already scarce plants, and the further loss of heathland itself, that grazing has been reintroduced.

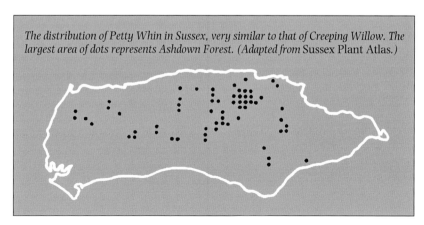

The distribution of Petty Whin in Sussex, very similar to that of Creeping Willow. The largest area of dots represents Ashdown Forest. (Adapted from Sussex Plant Atlas.*)*

The Forest woodlands and their plants

Although the various types of Forest woodlands are extensive, few are believed to be particularly old as significant areas were cleared for charcoal for the local iron industry. The commonest trees now, and perhaps the main components of the original Forest canopy, are Pedunculate Oak and Silver Birch, which in wetter areas are joined by species such as Alder (there is an old wood of this species above Newbridge), Downy Birch and the shrub Alder Buckthorn. Sessile Oak was probably much more common originally than it is today, in a few scattered sites on the Forest such as the ghyll north west of Duddleswell. Hazel is very common in the understorey of the more mature woodland. Since Holly can be common too, it is interesting to compare Coleman's observation in 1836 that 'little now remains except a dense thicket near Leg's Heath Gate'. In this area and eastwards towards the A22, there are some particularly fine stands of Beech. This species also marks many boundaries of land enclosed by the act of 1693. The conspicuous clumps of Scots Pine on the Forest were planted mainly in the nineteenth century. Like Silver Birch it can be an aggressive invader of the heathlands and requires careful control.

The floors of the older woodlands are the richest in plants, especially noticeable in spring and early summer before the trees have regained full leaf. Alongside the well-known Bluebell, Wood Anemone and Wood Sorrel, there are species still more characteristic of the Forest's poor soils. Bilberry (later with delicious purple berries) is out in April, its watery-pink bell-shaped flowers showing its close relationship to the heathers. In May Common Cowwheat comes into flower among the grasses whose roots it parasitizes. In June the Birds-nest Orchid appears beneath Beech; as it lacks any green pigment for photosynthesis, it has to obtain all the nutrients it needs from semi-decomposed leaf litter.

Rides through the trees provide both adequate light and disturbed ground for a selection of plants characteristic of the High Weald Forests of Ashdown, St Leonards and Worth, such as Ivy-leaved Bellflower and Lesser Skullcap. In damp ground there is an abundance of different ferns, including the Lemon-scented (or Mountain) Fern (a species mainly of western and northern Britain) and the rarer Marsh Fern. The latter is known from only a handful of Sussex sites, one of them being Alder woodland near Newbridge.

Ivy-leaved Bellflower.

*Beeches near the Beeches car park
(405316) above Twyford – spring.*

Birch against a winter sunset.

Fallow Deer does and young, Pippingford Park – September.

Fallow buck. Note the distinctive 'palmate' antlers.

Deer

Like other British forests, Ashdown owes its existence to deer; indeed the very word forest (as used by the French-speaking Normans) denotes a place of deer, where they could be hunted, rather than of trees. Place names like Hartfield and Hindleap emphasise the connection. Much of the outer limit of the present-day Forest boundary still follows the ancient pale whose stake-lined bank and ditch were built to allow deer to enter the Forest but not to leave it.

From the evidence of middens (refuse heaps), Red Deer were an essential part of culture in the Weald 6–8000 years ago. After the introduction of Fallow Deer by the Normans, both species were hunted in Ashdown Forest until the seventeenth century. They were managed by a Master Forester, or Master of the Game, and a team of assistants who had separate responsibilities for the Forest's three 'wards' and the six 'walks' within them. (Today's Forest Rangers similarly have their own 'chases'.) A 1539 survey recorded 300 Red and 7–800 Fallow Deer, only about a sixth of which were males (good evidence of the herds being managed). Perhaps because of the administrative chaos during and after the Civil War, the Red Deer declined and had disappeared by 1700. For no clear

Roe buck. Unlike Fallow Deer, Roe are not gregarious. Their parties consist usually of a doe and her fawns, sometimes accompanied by a buck.

The Fallow Deer logo of the Conservators of Ashdown Forest.

LEFT: *Deer reflectors on the Ridge Road, designed to warn deer of approaching traffic at night. They are believed to reduce casualties at certain well-used crossing points.*

reason the Fallow declined too over the next century. 'The last, a doe,' wrote the Rev. Edward Turner, Vicar of Maresfield, 'was accidentally sprung from a patch of brakes, just below Gills Lap, by the Hartfield and Withyham Harriers, while pursuing a hare, and after a run of two hours, killed, about the year 1808. Of this I was an eye-witness.'

Only the Fallow Deer have returned, having escaped probably from nearby Buckhurst Park in the early 1900s; they number now up to a thousand. For much of the year the does live on the Forest, often in large groups. The bucks, with new antlers, arrive from surrounding areas in September for the rut. Frayed saplings, patches of ground turned to mud and loud pig-like grunts and belches all indicate their return. In April they lose their antlers. In June and July the fawns are born. By the year's end about a hundred Fallow will have been killed on the roads, mainly on the A22 near Pippingford Park, their stronghold within Ashdown Forest.

While Fallow Deer are the most likely deer to be encountered, three other species occur on the Forest. Never apparently an important beast of the Forest, unlike the Red and Fallow Deer, the Roe is clearly on the increase in the 1990s. The tiny Muntjac (from China) is also increasing and there are occasional reports of Japanese Sika. The only Red Deer now are on the road signs!

Forest road sign showing Red Deer.

Autumn colour north of the Ridge Road.

Winter scene at Twyford.

Birds

Because birds are conspicuous, their changing fortunes on the Forest (as elsewhere) have been relatively well documented. Thus we know that in Cobbett's time the Black Grouse was abundant but within about 50 years it had died out – due almost certainly to the sort of agricultural improvements that he himself championed. The Raven had gone from inland Sussex by about 1880 (but its name lives on in Raven Wood at Pippingford; 432309) and the Red-backed Shrike, Woodlark and Curlew have been lost from the Forest since World War Two – although the last two may yet return as breeding birds.

A young Forest Nightjar on its nest near Old Lodge.

A male Redstart on the Forest.

By contrast, the early 1990s saw a remarkable resurgence of Britain's scarcest heathland species, the Dartford Warbler. Severe winters, however, can wipe out the entire Forest population. It breeds where gorse is well established among the heather, often alongside the Stonechat. Skylarks and Meadow Pipits occur particularly on the rides crossing the open heaths while species such as Linnets, Whitethroats, Reed Buntings and Yellowhammers are common where there is some scrub. There are a few pairs of Redpolls. The habitat of the Tree Pipit, a summer visitor only, is those parts of the heaths bordered or invaded by young Scots Pine and Silver Birch, from the top of which it launches into its song flight. The larger clumps of pines on the Forest can harbour pairs of Hobbys.

If any sound epitomises heathland in summer it is the extraordinary churring song of the Nightjar, uttered at dusk and accompanied by much gliding, swooping and the clapping of wings. By day, and on its nest, it sits still on a bare patch of ground among the heather and is almost impossible to find. From late February onwards, dusk is also the time for the Woodcock. In their roding display, the males fly steadily and evenly over the Forest woodlands uttering a curious croaking sound; only when crossing adjacent heathland, however, are they at all easy to see. The famous nineteenth century naturalist and field sportsman (and infamous egg collector) Charles St John recalled meeting a turnpike keeper in Ashdown Forest who 'used to kill two or three woodcock every evening for a week or two in March and April – shooting the birds while he smoked his pipe and drank his smuggled brandy and water'! In winter the heaths can seem almost birdless but there are usually one or two Hen Harriers and Great Grey Shrikes for the persevering bird-watcher to find.

Although the woodlands of the Forest hold birds of less national importance than do the heaths, there are breeding populations of species which are scarce elsewhere in south east England, such as the Redstart in groves of mature deciduous trees and the Wood Warbler which prefers close stands of Silver Birch. Many streams and ponds in the Forest have Grey Wagtails all year round and there is the occasional report of breeding Mandarin Duck (almost as common now in Britain as in its native eastern Asia).

Rare migrants do turn up too – but what does one make of the claim of Mr A.E. Knox that he saw two Pine Grosbeaks which had been killed on the Forest in February 1848? There have only been ten officially accepted records in Britain of this bird of the coniferous forests of northern Eurasia, and these were not two of them!

Dartford Warbler. In 1994 about 27 pairs were on Ashdown Forest.

Male Stonechat on the Forest, characteristically perching on top of gorse. Although many Stonechats leave the Forest in winter, a few usually remain.

Recent counts of some breeding birds (pairs or territories) in Sussex and Ashdown Forest. The percentage of the Sussex population occurring in the Forest is shown in brackets. (Data from *The Sussex Bird Report*.)

	Sussex	Ashdown Forest
Nightjar	148	39 (26%)
Tree Pipit	117	60 (51%)
Redstart	49	46 (94%)
Stonechat	63	44 (70%)

Other wildlife

Although many of the Forest's mammals, insects and other animals occur on almost any large expanse of semi-natural land, there are some heathland specialities worthy of mention.

This is particularly true of damselflies and dragonflies (the Odonata). Half of Britain's 46 breeding species have been recorded, the scarcer among them being the Black Darter, Brilliant Emerald and Small Red Damselfly. The best places to view them are on the Forest's few ponds, such as Ellison's Pond on the Stonehill Road (463287), the one at the Forest Centre, and those to the south of the Ridge Road between there and Coleman's Hatch (447329).

Of the Forest's 34 recorded species of butterflies, the most spectacular is the Purple Emperor but it can be hard to see. 'The Emperor', wrote a nineteenth century entomologist, 'invariably fixes his throne upon the summit of a lofty oak, from the utmost sprigs of which on sunny days he performs his aerial excursions, and in these he ascends to a much greater

The two red damselflies of Ashdown Forest. On the left is the Common Red Damselfly; it can be on the wing as early as April. On the right is the Small Red Damselfly which is a heathland speciality known, in Sussex, from just a few sites. It is slightly smaller than the Common Red, has red rather than black legs and appears first in June.

elevation than any other insect.' Equally elusive is the Purple Hairstreak which spends its entire adult life at the top of oak trees. On the woodland floors of the Forest, fritillaries have declined as they have in much of Britain where coppicing is no longer practised. Deep shade discourages the growth of violets on which their caterpillars depend for food. The Small Pearl-bordered Fritillary is recorded now from three sites on the Forest and the Pearl-bordered Fritillary from just one. The nationally rare

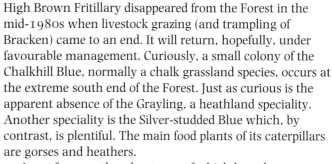

High Brown Fritillary disappeared from the Forest in the mid-1980s when livestock grazing (and trampling of Bracken) came to an end. It will return, hopefully, under favourable management. Curiously, a small colony of the Chalkhill Blue, normally a chalk grassland species, occurs at the extreme south end of the Forest. Just as curious is the apparent absence of the Grayling, a heathland speciality. Another speciality is the Silver-studded Blue which, by contrast, is plentiful. The main food plants of its caterpillars are gorses and heathers.

Apart from moths, about 400 of which have been recorded on the Forest, other insects and invertebrates are less well studied. As with plants, there are known to be some species which are more characteristic of the uplands of western Britain: examples are the beetle *Hydroporus longicornis* in *Sphagnum* pools and the spider *Centromerus arcanus*. Another speciality of pools is the Great Raft Spider (*Dolomedes fimbriatus*) which, at over five centimetres across, is one of Britain's largest and quite capable of catching small fish!

Although plentiful on the Forest heathlands, Adders are seldom seen since they tend to disappear when they detect people approaching. They should be of little concern as long as they are left alone. Grass Snakes are less common. The nationally rare Smooth Snake and Sand Lizard, both characteristic species of the New Forest and the Dorset heathlands, do not occur on Ashdown.

Silver-studded Blue. It is (or rather the males are) the smallest British blue butterfly with mainly blue uppersides to the wings.

Management

The Ashdown Forest Act 1974, Section 16, states: 'It shall be the duty of the Conservators . . . to regulate and manage the Forest as an amenity and place of resort subject to the existing rights of common . . . and to protect such rights . . . (and) . . . the Forest from encroachments and to conserve it as a quiet and natural area of outstanding beauty.' For an ancient, man-made landscape like Ashdown Forest to survive and be appreciated in modern times, persistent efforts are required by a host of people – not just the Conservators and Forest Rangers, but also estate workers, scientists, the Commoners, conservation organisations and volunteers. Other levels of protection are given by the Forest's position within the High Weald Area of Outstanding Natural Beauty and by its status as a Site of Special Scientific Interest. European legislation may add further protection.

The importance of heathland for wildlife means that its management and conservation are a top priority. Traditionally it was maintained by practices such as grazing, the cutting of wood for fuel and the removal of litter for animal bedding. Substitutes are provided now by a combination of the tractor-driven mower, mechanical digger, chain saw and even herbicide (to prevent resprouting of birch stumps).

Some Commoners still collect estovers but large-scale removal of Forest products has effectively ceased. Deliberate burning of heathland, to provide a flush of new grass for grazing and to kill ticks that parasitise livestock, is now a less frequent form of management that favoured the spread and dominance of Bracken. Bracken is a resilient plant whose system of spreading rhizomes is underground, protected from fire and frost, and whose leaves alone grow above ground. The best way to control it is by mowing in June and again in July – which practice eventually weakens the rhizomes. Currently about 60 hectares are mown every year. Other obvious problems associated with burning are danger and the unappealing charred landscape that results; less obvious is the destructive effect it has on wildlife such as insects and other invertebrates.

Sheep flock in the fenced enclosure at Millbrook (1994).

Management policy is to mow heather on a 15-year cycle to encourage a mosaic of differently-aged patches, and to check the invasion of heathland by trees. Many studies have shown, however, that mowing on a large scale is not only more expensive but also less efficient than grazing in achieving these aims. A report commissioned in 1985 recommended the introduction of enclosed grazing to the Forest heathlands. Understandable alarm at the fencing required led to exhaustive consult-

British Trust for Conservation Volunteers clearing Silver Birch from heathland by the Ridge Road. The views are opened up north towards East Grinstead and the North Downs.

ations with the public and countryside organisations to provide reassurance about ease of access and the unobtrusive nature of the fences themselves. A pilot scheme at Millbrook with a 40-hectare enclosure containing sheep and Welsh Black cattle proved successful and in 1994 approval was sought from the Department of the Environment (in accordance with the Ashdown Forest Act 1974) for a further 445 hectares to be fenced and grazed. The aim of this, as with previous measures, is to save and enhance the remaining heathland, to prevent it being lost to Bracken, scrub and trees, and to conserve the wildlife that occurs there and nowhere else. The end result will also be a partial recreation of a traditional pastoral landscape now sadly rare. (The Sussex Wildlife Trust already grazes sheep at its Old Lodge Local Nature Reserve; the entrance is at 469307.)

The woodlands too are managed, by following traditional techniques. Coppicing involves cutting down trees and shrubs and allowing the remaining stumps to resprout. The harvesting of the new growth on a regular cycle was once an activity of great economic (and ecological) importance. Coppicing now can meet the demands of conservation as well as provide a source of income for woodland products, such as Hazel hurdles. Some areas contain stands of coppiced Sweet Chestnut which produces a rapid growth of straight and easily split poles used for the traditional post-and-rail style of Sussex fencing. Simultaneously, the thinning of scrub and low quality trees (such as the Scots Pines sold as Christmas trees) encourages the growth of straight-trunked oak 'standards' for high quality timber.

There are, of course, innumerable other tasks such as clearing thickets of Rhododendron (an invasive, exotic species), surveying wildlife, acquiring land within the old pale (such as 32 hectares at Chelwood Vachery in 1994), putting out fires and dealing with deer casualties on the roads. There is more, however, to Forest management than physical work alone. In their determination of Forest management, the Board of Conservators have to consider the Forest's position in the crowded South East within a context of local policies and politics; threats need to be recognised and rebuffed; and long-term plans need formulation for retaining the Forest's characteristic landscape, wildlife, and role in public recreation.

FAR RIGHT: *Walkers in the woodlands below Chelwood Vachery.*

Sweet Chestnut being coppiced on the south side of the Ridge Road.

Looking northwards to East Grinstead from the Broadstone car park on the Ridge Road.

Watching the horses near Camp Hill.

Leisure

Walking and enjoying the views are the main leisure activties on the Forest so a large part of the Forest's resources are devoted to maintaining rides, footpaths and car parks. Many of the 50 or so car parks are on the higher parts of the Forest and command fine views towards the North and South Downs. On a hot summer's day they can teem with people and cars! A short walk, however, can take you to where it is quiet. Riding is by permit only (from the Forest Centre) or with local riding stables; mountain bikes are not allowed.

Nutley Windmill

Just as the iron industry harnessed water power in the lower parts of the Forest, so windmills exploited wind power on higher ground to grind the corn of smallholders. One of the best preserved of the 80 or so surviving in Sussex stands just north of the Nutley to Duddleswell road at an elevation of 155 metres (451291). Now somewhat sheltered by vegetation, it was probably far more exposed in 1836 when it was first recorded from the site, 20 metres outside the post-1693 Forest boundary. Parts of it may be about 300 years old. It represents a basic early form of the English post-mill, so called because the entire structure revolves around a post to face the wind. It has been restored to the full working order it lost in 1908 and is managed by the Uckfield and District Preservation Society. The mill is open at least on the last Sunday of each month from April to October.

Nutley Windmill.

The Airman's Grave.

The Airman's Grave

Early in the morning of 31 July 1941, a Wellington bomber of 142 Squadron crashed on the Forest on its return from a raid on Cologne; all six crew died. The site is marked by a memorial (not, in fact, a grave) on a heathland ride west of Duddleswell (458276; marked AIRMEN'S GRAVE).

Winnie the Pooh

Of all Ashdown Forest's visitors and inhabitants, the one most closely associated with it is Winnie the Pooh, many of whose adventures took place around Gills Lap. Just north of there are both The Enchanted Place (468319) and a memorial to the author A.A. Milne (who lived and worked in Hartfield) and E.H. Shepard, the illustrator. Pooh Sticks Bridge (471338) is about 600 metres outside the Forest boundary and is best approached from the Pooh car park (472332) just west of Chuck Hatch. The original Winnie was a Black Bear that was brought to London Zoo by a Canadian soldier, Lt Colebourn, in 1914 and was visited by Milne and his son, Christopher Robin. Winnie is apparently short for Winnipeg, the soldier's home town.

Ashdown Forest Centre

The Ashdown Forest Centre, just east of Wych Cross, is the administrative and logistic base for the Forest. It was completed in 1983 and consists of three old reconstructed barns. Named after the Roman word for their castle at Pevensey, the Anderida Barn is the only one from Sussex (from near Hassocks) and houses the Centre's exhibition area. As well as a permanent display interpreting the Forest for visitors, there is also an area for shorter viewings, often of local craftwork or relating to some topic of seasonal interest. In a separate building there are educational facilities and material for school parties. Originally the Centre's roof was thatched with heather in traditional style.

Christopher Robin and Winnie the bear at London Zoo in 1921.

A 1929 watercolour, by A.E. Rowe, of the Forest, looking west towards Camp Hill.

References and recommended reading

Christian, G. (1967). *Ashdown Forest*. The Society of the Friends of Ashdown Forest, Forest Row.

Cleere, H. and Crossley, D. (1985). *The Iron Industry of the Weald*. Leicester University Press, Leicester.

Hall, P.C. (1980). *Sussex Plant Atlas*. Booth Museum of Natural History, Borough of Brighton. Also the *Selected Supplement* by M. Briggs (1990).

Irons, J.K. (1982). *Aspects of the Impact of Man on the Historical Ecology of Ashdown Forest, Sussex, before 1885*. Ph.D. dissertation, University of Sussex, Brighton.

Robinson, D.A. and Williams, R.B.G. (1984). Landform Guides No. 4: *Classic Landforms of the Weald*. The Geographical Association, Sheffield, in association with the British Geomorphological Research Group.

The Geography Editorial Committee, University of Sussex (1983). *Sussex: Environment, Landscape and Society*. Alan Sutton Publishing Ltd, Gloucester.

The Sussex Ornithological Society (annual). *The Sussex Bird Report*.

Willard, B. (1989). *The Forest: Ashdown in East Sussex*. Sweethaws Press, Uckfield.

For brevity, scientific names of wildlife have generally not been used. English names follow those found in most modern field guides.

The Society of the Friends of Ashdown Forest

This Society supports the work of the Conservators by fund-raising. Members receive a magazine, *Ashdown Forest News*, which contains articles on a wide range of subjects relating to the Forest. There is a stone-mounted memorial plaque on the Forest to the Society's founder chairman, Bob Lumsden, near the Sharpthorne to Forest Row road (407333). To join, contact the Ashdown Forest Centre, Wych Cross, Forest Row, East Sussex RH18 5JP.

The authors

Both authors are Commoners of Ashdown Forest. PHILIP GLYN has a veterinary practice in the area and HEW PRENDERGAST works at the Royal Botanic Gardens, Kew.

ACKNOWLEDGEMENTS

For their varied help we are very grateful to the Board of Conservators and to: Brig. Mike Constantine, Stephen Dalton, Chris Marrable, Dr D.A. Martin, Madeline and Peter Reader, Dr Tim Rich, Margaret Tebbutt, Dr Rendel Williams, East Sussex County Records Office, Lewes and the Headquarters, Cinque Ports Training Area. For the use of illustrative material we thank also: the Conservators of Ashdown Forest (pp.11, 15); Earl de la Warr (p.8); Peter Kirby (p.9); Dr Gerald Legg (Booth Museum of Natural History, map p.17); Phil Lucas (Danehill Parish Historical Society, p.14 top); Mr and Mrs B. Mead (p.35); Mary Prendergast (p.21 bottom); Zoological Society of London (p.34). We acknowledge the writings of previous researchers on the Forest, especially the late C.F. Tebbutt.

All photographs are by the authors except for: Alan Barnes (NHPA, p.25); John Buckingham (NHPA, p.24 left); Stephen Dalton (NHPA, front cover and title page); Dr Peter Gasson (p.27); and Chris Marrable (pp.18, 21 top, 24 right, 30). The paintings are by Jane Peschiera (pp.4, 25, 26) and the maps are by Joanne Way (inside front cover, pp.7, 17, 32 and 33).

We are particularly indebted to Elwyn Blacker and the staff at Pardoe Blacker Publishing.

First published by ESSEDON PRESS
Cherry Garden Farm · Ivydene Lane
Ashurst Wood · West Sussex RH19 3TN.

Designed by Pardoe Blacker Limited, Lingfield, Surrey.
Printed by Ghyllprint Limited, Heathfield, Sussex.